MYSTERIES OF THE DEEP

John Townsend

www.raintreepublishers.co.uk

Visit our website to find out more information about **Raintree** books.

To order:

 Phone 44 (0) 1865 888113

 Send a fax to 44 (0) 1865 314091

Visit the Raintree Bookshop at **www.raintreepublishers.co.uk** to browse our catalogue and order online.

First published in Great Britain by Raintree Publishers, Halley Court, Jordan Hill, Oxford OX2 8EJ, part of Harcourt Education Ltd.
Raintree is a registered trademark of Harcourt Education Ltd.

Editorial: Charlotte Guillain and Isabel Thomas
Design: Michelle Lisseter and Bridge Creative Services Ltd
Picture Research: Maria Joannou and Kay Altwegg
Production: Jonathan Smith

Originated by Ambassador
Printed and bound in China and Hong Kong by South China

ISBN 1 844 43222 X
08 07 06 05 04
10 9 8 7 6 5 4 3 2 1

British Library Cataloguing in Publication Data
Townsend, John, 1924–
Mysteries of the deep. – (Out there)
1. Sea monsters – Juvenile literature
2. Curiosities and wonders – Juvenile literature
001.9'44

A full catalogue record for this book is available from the British Library.

Acknowledgements
Page 04–05, NHPA/; 05 top, Robert Harding/; 05 mid, Corbis/; 05 bott, NHPA/Agence Nature; 06–07, Topham Picturepoint/; 06, Corbis/; 07, Getty Images; 08–09, Robert Harding/; 08, Photodisc/; 09, Corbis/; 10–11, /Wm Leo Smith ; 11, Corbis/; 12–13, Mary Evans Picture Library/; 12, Corbis/; 13, Wade Pemberton/; 14–15, Photodisc/; 14, Corbis/; 15, Ancient Egypt Picture Library/; 14–15, Mary Evans Picture Library/; 16–17, Robert Harding/; 17, Corbis/; 18–19, Corbis/Photo Library Ltd; 19, Corbis/; 20–21, Corbis/; 21, Mary Evans Picture Library/ ; 20, Corbis/; 22, Hulton Archives/; 22–23, Corbis/; 23, Photodisc/; 24–25, Ronald Grant Archives; 24, Mary Evans Picture Library/; 26–27, Corbis/; 26, Corbis/; 27, Corbis/; 28, Corbis/; 28–29, Corbis/; 29, Corbis/; 30, Photodisc/; 31, Mary Evans Picture Library/; 32–33, NHPA/; 32, Corbis/; 33, Corbis/; 34–35, Corbis/; 35, Corbis/; 36–37, NHPA/Pete Atkinson; 36, Corbis/; 37, Corbis/; 38–39, NHPA/Norbert Wu; 38, Kim Reisenbichler/Monterey Bay Aquarium Research Institute; 38–39, NHPA/Agence Nature; 41, NHPA/A.N.T; 40–41, NHPA/A.N.T; 40, NHPA/A.N.T; 42, Corbis/; 43, Nature Picture Library/; 42–43, Ronald Grant Archives/; 44–45, NHPA/Pete Atkinson; 45, NHPA/; 44, NHPA/; 46–47, FLPA/; 46, NHPA/; 47, Ronald Grant Archives/; 48–49, Corbis/; 48, Corbis/; 49, Corbis/; 50–51, Photodisc/; 50, Corbis/. Cover photograph reproduced with permission of Still Pictures.

Every effort has been made to contact copyright holders of any material reproduced in this book. Any omissions will be rectified in subsequent printings if notice is given to the publishers.

Disclaimer
All the Internet addresses (URLs) given in this book were valid at the time of going to press. However, due to the dynamic nature of the Internet, some addresses may have changed, or sites may have changed or ceased to exist since publication. While the author and Publishers regret any inconvenience this may cause readers, no responsibility for any such changes can be accepted by either the author or the Publishers.

CONTENTS

Any words appearing in the text in bold, **like this,** are explained in the Glossary. You can also look out for them in the Weird words box at the bottom of each page.

THE GREAT UNKNOWN

The oceans of the world are full of secrets. Will we ever really know what is hidden in their depths? Undersea mountains, canyons and caves could hide another world. Scientists think there are millions of creatures they do not yet know about in the mud at the bottom of the seas.

THE DEEPEST SEAS

This table shows the Earth's deepest bodies of water.

There are even deeper **trenches** and undersea caves that no one has explored.

SECRET WORLD

From the time people first set sail in ships they had to cope with the great power of the sea. Sailors told stories of its magic, its moods, its monsters and its mystery. But even now it is hard to imagine the real size of the oceans. The Pacific Ocean alone holds half the world's water. It holds thousands of lost ships, too.

SEA	DEEPEST PARTS
Pacific Ocean	10,924 metres
Atlantic Ocean	9219 metres
Indian Ocean	7455 metres
Caribbean Sea	6946 metres
Arctic Ocean	5625 metres

lurk   wait around, ready to strike
seabed   floor at the bottom of the sea

DEEP BLUE SEA

Seventy per cent of the Earth is made up of water. Some of it is as deep as 28 Empire State Buildings standing on top of each other. It can be so cold and dark in places that no one has ever been down to the bottom. In fact, more people have been up into space than down into the deepest ocean. The pressure of the water would crush you to death in seconds. But now cameras and special submarines can dive very deep to show us what hides on the **seabed**.

The 21st century will be a time of discovery as we start to explore more of the mysteries of the deep.

A blue whale's mouth is so huge, a football team could stand on its tongue!

FIND OUT LATER...

Do secrets still lie in the wrecks at the bottom of the sea?

Are there really great powers locked in the oceans?

*What kinds of creatures **lurk** in the depths of the sea?*

trench   deep ditch, gully or valley

SEA GODS

The Romans believed Neptune was the god who ruled the sea. If they upset him, their ship would sink. For the Greeks, it was a god called Poseidon they had to please. The sea's storms and scary creatures were all thought to be controlled by the gods.

The sea has always terrified people who have had to sail in its storms. Sailors in **ancient** Greece used to believe they had to please the gods to make the sea stay calm. Even today there are more **superstitions** about the sea than anything else.

THE KRAKEN

Myths and story-telling over hundreds of years have added to the sea's mystery. Tales like the kraken from Norway still amaze us. The **Vikings** were early sailors who told of a huge sea monster that looked like a giant octopus. The kraken could sink any ship and eat everyone on board. The kraken could even suck a whole ship down into the sea.

OLD IDEAS

When sailors thought the world was flat, they were in constant fear of falling off the edge of the Earth. They thought that if they sailed too far, they would reach the land of the devil. Or maybe they would meet Neptune, the god of the sea. Meeting Neptune was thought to bring certain death. And where did Neptune live… in the Sargasso Sea. That is in the middle of the Bermuda Triangle, a place known for its danger even today.

Many Roman statues show Neptune, god of the sea. **‹‹**

WEIRD WORDS

myth made-up tale, told over many years
omen sign that may bring good or evil

BAD LUCK

Sailors often felt they were in danger and needed luck. But many things were thought to bring bad luck. If a cross-eyed woman looked at a ship, she was bound to bring disaster.

Cats were kept on ships to kill rats and bring luck.

BELIEFS

The ship's cat could be an **omen**. Black cats have always been linked with luck. But they were said to bring storms if they cleaned their paws within sight of a ship. If a live rabbit ever went on board, the ship was doomed.

Pictures of the kraken have been drawn from sailors' stories.

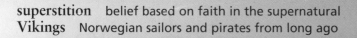

superstition   belief based on faith in the supernatural
Vikings   Norwegian sailors and pirates from long ago

THE FAMOUS MERMAID

The Little Mermaid of Copenhagen is Denmark's most famous statue. The Danish writer Hans Christian Andersen told the story of the daughter of the Sea King. She lived in the deepest sea 'where the sea people live'. The story says that she saved a prince from drowning.

MYTH AND LEGEND

Sailors have told tales of strange sea creatures that have puzzled the world for years. But are these stories from sailors' imaginations, or even tricks of the mind? Many sailors swear they have really seen **mermaids** in the ocean.

MERMAIDS

Mermaids have been part of sailors' **folklore** for centuries. Can there really be creatures in the ocean with the head and body of a human and the tail of a large fish? There have been many reports of mermaids from all around the world for hundreds of years. Sailors used to dread seeing a mermaid, as it was a sure sign that their ship would run into trouble.

mermaid   sea creature with the body of a beautiful woman and the tail of a fish

ALIVE AND WELL?

For years, people have reported seeing mermaids off the coast of Hawaii. In 1998 someone claimed to have taken a photo of the Kaiwi Point Mermaid. He said, 'She had long flowing hair and one of the most beautiful faces I've ever seen.' So even today some people believe mermaids really exist.

SIRENS

A **siren** was a beautiful creature that was half woman and half bird. She was said to sing so sweetly that sailors would go into a **trance**. They would dive into the sea to be with her and then they would drown. Or the siren's singing would make sailors steer their ship into the deadly rocks.

THE MANATEE

Anyone seeing a manatee for the first time would be puzzled. These large, gentle mammals are grey with pink patches on their skin. Perhaps from a distance they look like mermaids?

Maybe sailors mistook seals, dolphins or manatees for mermaids. ⌄⌄

siren   beautiful creature in Greek myths, whose singing attracted sailors

SERPENTS OF THE DEEP

Some books describe a monster as 'an animal of strange or terrifying shape and very large for its kind'. In that case, the sea is home to some real monsters. But we are still not certain whether giant sea serpents exist.

FEAR OF THE UNKNOWN

Before people knew about some of the world's real sea creatures, they must have been scared whenever a fin or tail splashed to the surface of the sea. It is easy to see why sailors believed in weird beasts. Even today, there are reports of USOs, as some sailors call them. These are Unidentified Swimming Objects – like **UFOs** that appear in the sea.

SNAKE OF THE SEA

The most common USO reported over the years is like a giant sea **serpent**. Many reports describe huge, dark sea snakes 50 metres long. Some have a 'seaweed-like **mane**' and fierce staring eyes. They could still be out there.

larva   young creature just after it has hatched
mane   long hair growing down the neck

CLOSE ENCOUNTER

A ship called the *Hilary* was sailing near Iceland in 1917. A creature with a head like a cow and a body 20 metres long suddenly rose from the sea. The sailors shot at it and the creature sank without trace. They never knew if they hit it or if it dived back into the sea to live another day.

THE OARFISH

Could an oarfish be mistaken for a sea serpent? It is one of the strangest looking fish. It has a silver body and a bright red mane that runs down its back. Oarfish live in deep seas and only come up to the surface when they are sick.

Some oarfish grow to be 20 metres long.

Large eels can be some of the scariest sea creatures.

serpent   like a large snake
UFO   Unidentified Flying Object

LOST BELOW THE WAVES

THE SARGASSO SEA

The Sargasso Sea near the island of Bermuda has thick seaweed. Large eels come here from all around the world to **spawn**. The rich weed protects their eggs. Why does the weed grow so much here? Some say it is fed by Atlantis deep below.

Stories are often told about a rich land full of gold and jewels. It was a fine city that was at the heart of a great **continent** until it sank forever. It is believed the city is now deep beneath the sea. Many people have tried to find it. The Greek writer Plato first wrote about the lost land of Atlantis in 350 BC.

ATLANTIS

Why did the sea drown Atlantis? Did sea levels suddenly rise? Was there an earthquake or a giant wave? Many **legends** describe a great flood about 11,000 years ago, when volcanoes and storms hit the Earth. Maybe the water rose too high and drowned Atlantis.

Feeding on the lost world? Parts of the Sargasso Sea are 7000 metres deep.

continent   large land mass – bigger than an island
fate   power that controls what will happen

WHERE?

Atlantis remains one of the sea's great mysteries. Of all the world's unsolved puzzles, the **fate** of Atlantis is especially strange. Apart from the question 'Did Atlantis really exist?' we want to know where it was. And where is it now?

Some people say the lost land is now far below the ice of Antarctica. Others believe it is in the middle of the Indian Ocean. But the mysterious Sargasso Sea around Bermuda may hold more secrets. This is the area of the Bermuda Triangle, where many boats have gone missing. Perhaps Atlantis lies at the bottom of the Sargasso Sea. With its strange mists and thick seaweed it would stay hidden for ever.

Is this part of a 'lost world' under the sea?

THE ROAD TO ATLANTIS

Near the Sargasso Sea there is a strange line of stones a third of a kilometre long beneath the sea. This 'pathway' was found in 1968 near the Bimini Islands. Some say it is just a **rock formation** but others think this 'Bimini Road' leads to Atlantis.

A painting of what Atlantis may have looked like. ◀◀

---

rock formation natural feature made by the wearing away or movement of rock

Melting glaciers are raising the sea level all the time.

SINKING

Many lands have vanished beneath the sea. Some old maps of the Pacific Ocean show islands that no longer exist. Earthquakes can make land fall into the sea. But more often the sea rises slowly, metre by metre, as ice at the poles melts. Streets and buildings could be lost forever.

SUNK

The land of Lemuria was said to be the Garden of Eden where the human race began. Now it is thought to lie below the Indian Ocean. Another land called Mu may have been drowned by the Pacific Ocean. Its story was told on **ancient stone tablets**, hidden in a **Hindu** temple.

THE END OF AN AGE

Many islands were doomed when warmer weather ended the Ice Age. Melting ice fell into the sea and the water level rose. In many places it has been rising ever since. Many towns by the sea have been destroyed. Old Dunwich in the UK was drowned. Some say its church bells still clang below the waves.

Divers hope to find lost treasure.

Hindu   belonging to the ancient Indian religion of Hinduism

ALEXANDRIA, EGYPT

The Lighthouse of Alexandria was a magnificent tower built above the Egyptian rocks for all to see. It guided sailors for sixteen centuries. It saved many from drowning but it could not save itself. It crashed into the sea hundreds of years ago when an earthquake struck. Part of the city of Alexandria fell into the ocean with the lighthouse.

FOUND

In 1934, a huge marble head from a statue of Alexander the Great was lifted from the water. Alexander was the famous leader who built the city. Local fishermen had known about its lost buildings for years. They used to swim through the undersea ruins.

PORT ROYAL, JAMAICA

Just before noon on 7 June 1692, an earthquake hit the West Indies. Much of Kingston Harbour in Jamaica fell into the sea.

About 2000 people were killed in an instant.

Divers have since found shops and pubs in the underwater streets.

A marble statue from Alexandria has been rescued from the **seabed**. ᗕᗕ

stone tablets slabs of stone that are carved with writing

AUSTRALIA'S 'SHIPWRECK COAST'

Hundreds of wrecks lie in the sands off the coast of Victoria, Australia. Ships full of silver or spices met their end on the rocks in storms. The first was the *Tryall* in 1622. Since then, over 700 ships have been lost along this rocky coast.

GOLD AND SILVER

Many people love to hear stories of sunken treasure. The **seabed** could be hiding many treasure chests packed with fine things. Ships used to carry all kinds of riches. There are thousands of wrecks in the oceans and many have never been found.

FLORIDA

Off the coast of Florida is a ships' graveyard. Storms here have smashed many boats against the **reefs** over the years. In 1715, ten Spanish ships sank in one night. As well as tobacco and sugar, they were carrying treasure. An eleventh ship, the *Urca de Lima*, **survived** the storm and saved all its gold and silver coins – until it sank in the next night's storm.

Scuba divers can explore the wrecks off the Australian coast.

dreaded   feared
fleet   large group of ships

VICTIMS OF THE ANGRY SEA

In July 1733, another Spanish **fleet** of treasure ships came to a watery end off the Florida coast. More than twenty ships were full of treasures taken from the American **continent**. The ships were taking gold and spices back to Spain. They had just left Cuba when the storm struck a **dreaded** area of sea that is famous for hurricanes. Today it is called the Bermuda Triangle.

Before they could get to shelter, the ships were smashed by giant waves. Only one ship escaped. The others were scattered and wrecked along the Upper Florida Keys. The wrecks stayed there for over 200 years. Modern-day treasure hunters have now **looted** them all.

▶ ▶ ▶ ▶ ▶ ▶ ▶ ▶ ▶ ▶ ▶

Find out more about the Bermuda Triangle on page 30.

FULL-TIME TREASURE HUNTER

Robert Ballard's job is finding sunken ships. One of his projects has found ships in the Black Sea that are over 1500 years old. He also looks for clues about great floods, like those of Noah's Ark – and maybe Atlantis.

Robert Ballard (centre) has discovered some of the oldest shipwrecks, including the *Titanic*. ❱❱

looted   raided
reef   ridge of rock or coral near the surface of the sea

MYSTERY SHIPS

GUARD AGAINST GHOST SHIPS

There were many **superstitions** that sailors thought would help keep their ships safe.

Sailors had a lot to be afraid of, including sea creatures, storms and dangerous rocks. Yet sea journeys could be calm and usually took many days. Sounds and shapes in the mist would stir sailors' imaginations.

LOOK OUT!

Each ship was said to have a **soul**. Sailors believed that if a ship sank, its soul would keep sailing the seas. That is how sailors explained some of the ghostly shapes they saw in the fog. But if they met a ghost ship, it was bad news. It meant the sailors were doomed and they would never see land again.

Nail horseshoes to ships' masts for protection.

Break a bottle to launch a ship. This is an offering to the gods for protection.

Do not carry a black bag on to a ship. It is bad luck.

To pass the time, sailors often told mysterious stories.

THE *FLYING DUTCHMAN*

An old sea **legend** told of a Dutch sea captain whose ship met a storm off the coast of South Africa. The Cape of Good Hope is famous for its stormy seas and the captain feared he would drown. He screamed a **curse**: 'I WILL get round this Cape even if I have to sail forever!'

THE CURSE

Ever since, sailors say they have seen the *Flying Dutchman* adrift in storms. It was meant to be bad luck for anyone who saw the ghost ship. No sailor would sail on any ship that had met the *Flying Dutchman*. It became a curse of the seas.

THE CAPE OF GOOD HOPE

The Cape of Good Hope is at the southern tip of Africa, where winds and high waves meet with great force. It was once called the Cape of Storms. Many ships have met a violent end here and sailors **dread** these waters.

The sea off the coast of South Africa can be deadly in a storm, even for modern boats.

THE FREEZING SEA

Old sailing ships in Arctic waters had dangers other than icebergs. Their masts and decks would clog up with ice and snow. This would make them top-heavy. **Whaling ships** were often wrecked in icy storms around Baffin Island in the North Atlantic.

GHOSTLY TALE

Mystery surrounds a ship called the *Rescue*. In 1860 it met another American ship in a storm near Baffin Island in the North Atlantic. The *Rescue* was in great danger so the crew climbed aboard the larger ship called the *George Henry* just in time. The next day the *Rescue* had vanished.

A year later the *George Henry* was back near Baffin Island and its sailors reported a strange sight. From out of the icy mist, the *Rescue* appeared again and scraped past. Its decks were full of snow as it creaked and drifted on through the icebergs.

Sailors say the icy ship still haunts the North Atlantic today.

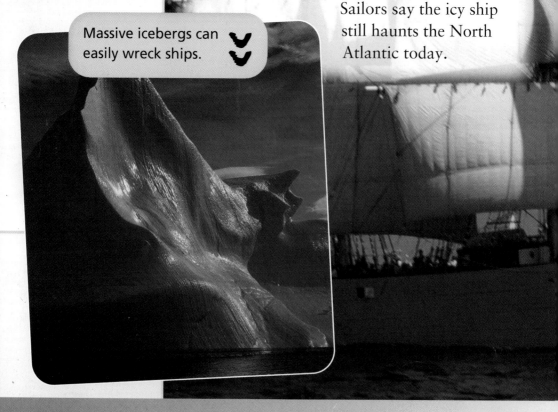

Massive icebergs can easily wreck ships.

New World   the Americas, which were just being discovered

PHANTOM SAILOR

Joseph Slocum was famous for being the first man to sail alone around the world. It took him three years. He left Boston in the USA in 1895 in his boat the *Spray*. A storm blew for days and Joseph fought to keep his boat from sinking. Worn out, he fell asleep. When he woke up, the *Spray* was gliding through huge waves. On deck he saw an old sailor steering the boat. Joseph was sure a ghost had come to save him.

In 1909 Joseph set sail from Massachusetts for South America. He was 65 when he left and he was never seen again. No one knows what happened to him.

Joseph Slocum saw a **phantom** sailor steering his boat through a storm.

WHO WAS THE SHADOWY FIGURE?

The mysterious figure wore clothes from the 15th century and said he was from the *Pinta*. That was one of Christopher Columbus's ships that sailed in 1492 to find the **New World**.

phantom   ghostly appearance
whaling ship   ship used for hunting whales

THE U-65 SUBMARINE MYSTERY

How could one submarine have so much back luck?

* On the first sea trial, the engine room filled with fumes and killed three men.

* In calm sea, a man fell overboard and was lost.

* Just after a priest tried to get rid of the jinx, a gunner went mad and an engineer broke his leg.

THE HAUNTED U-BOAT

Even before the German submarine U-65 sailed in World War One, it had bad luck. An officer was one of ten men killed when a **torpedo** exploded while they were loading it. Soon afterwards sailors saw the officer's ghost standing on deck. Then the submarine captain was killed during a battle. What else could happen to this **jinxed** submarine?

More accidents happened to men on the submarine. None could be explained. Then in 1918, an enemy US submarine saw the U-65. Before the American captain could take aim, he saw a lone figure standing on the U-65's deck. Suddenly, the jinxed German U-boat mysteriously exploded and sank.

This German submarine was doomed.

jinx   unlucky force
retired   no longer in active service

THE HAUNTED AIRCRAFT CARRIER

In July 1967, the aircraft carrier USS *Forrestal* was off the coast of Vietnam. A Phantom Jet on deck let off a rocket by mistake. The rocket hit the fuel tank of another jet. Suddenly the whole deck was covered in flames. Fuel tanks and bombs exploded and many men were blown overboard. Others were trapped below deck and burned to death. More than 130 men lost their lives and the ship needed massive repairs.

After that, strange things happened on board the *Forrestal* before it **retired** in 1993. Voices, doors opening, 'ghostly hands' and flickering lights led people to believe a ghost was on board. They called the ghost 'George'.

The USS *Forrestal* was over 300 metres long, with 19 levels.

THE USS FORRESTAL

The USS *Forrestal* was big enough to hide a ghost. It was said that 'George' often touched sailors and even gripped one for a while. A man reported that a disused phone kept ringing. He answered it and heard a cry for help.

torpedo   cigar-shaped underwater missile

DISASTER

UNSINKABLE

The *Titanic*'s owners said the ship was so safe that it did not need many lifeboats. The chances of the ship sinking were said to be one in a million. Yet 23 passengers cancelled their tickets and told others they thought the ship was doomed.

Many mysteries surround the **maiden voyage** of the *Titanic*. It sank to the icy depths of the North Atlantic at 2:20 a.m. on 15 April 1912. 1513 men, women and children were lost. The world was stunned by the news. Just how could this happen when it had been built to be unsinkable?

STRANGE PASSENGER

One mystery was why William Stead was on board. A number of people reported his story afterwards. He had made a fuss about the number of lifeboats on the *Titanic*. He did not think there were enough. He turned out to be right, but he still set sail.

WHITE STAR LINE

T.S.S. TITANIC.

Titanic Facts

Total **capacity**: 3320 people
Number of lifeboats: 20
Lifeboat capacity: 1178 people
Top speed: 25 knots
Passengers onboard: 2224
Number of survivors: 705

These *Titanic* postcards were never used. ❮❮

capacity   number that can fit onboard
maiden voyage   first journey

WARNINGS

A **psychic** had warned Stead not to sail on the *Titanic*. He had other warnings from strangers. One woman told him he would 'soon be called home'. It was later said that as the *Titanic* sailed out of Southampton, a woman in the crowd cried, 'That ship is going to sink! Do something! Save them!'

TRAGEDY

Four days later, the great ship hit an iceberg. There were too few lifeboats to save all of the 2224 passengers and crew. William Stead was among the 1513 people who died. It is hard to imagine what his last thoughts must have been as the ship went down.

JUST LIKE THE *TITANIC* . . .

In 1898, 14 years before the *Titanic* sank, Morgan Robertson wrote a book about a ship named the *Titan*.

In the story, *Titan*:
- was British and sailed in April
- had a top speed of 25 knots
- had just over 2000 passengers
- hit an iceberg and sank with heavy loss of life.

The *Titanic* was the world's largest ocean liner.

psychic someone able to see the future and show unusual powers of the mind

The *Titanic's* captain believed the ship was unsinkable.

> I cannot imagine an event that would cause a ship to **flounder**. Modern ship building has gone beyond that.
>
> E.J. Smith,
> Titanic Captain.

THE WRECK OF THE *TITANIC*

For years it was a big mystery. Just where was the wreck of the *Titanic*?

It took over 70 years to find the wreck. Experts knew roughly where it was, but for years it was too far down for divers to reach. At last, **sonar** images showed solid shapes on the **seabed**. The scientist and diver Robert Ballard and his team found the *Titanic* in 1985. They had been searching for five years. The submarine dives helped show how the *Titanic* sank. The ship had gone down fast. It had split in two as it sank. The wreck lies in two parts, torn between the third and fourth **funnels**.

This photo of the first-class area was taken just before the *Titanic* sailed.

coral   hard undersea growth around tiny sea creatures
flounder   struggle

SILENT WORLD

Cameras and mini-subs have filmed the wreck lying in metres of mud. The anchors, the rails and the funnels are all still there. A light fitting from the grand staircase is still in one piece, with **coral** growing out of it.

All human remains have gone. The water and mud on the seabed contained enough acid to destroy bodies and bones over time. Robert Ballard made seven dives before leaving a **plaque** in memory of those who lost their lives that night in 1912.

The wreck of the *Titanic* is now left alone as a lasting grave to the hundreds of people who died.

MYSTERIES

Many **rumours** said something else sank the *Titanic*.

- A crashed spaceship was said to lie near the wreck.
- An Egyptian mummy was said to be in the hold, being taken to a museum in New York. Did the mummy's **curse** sink the ship?

The *Titanic* rests just off the coast of Newfoundland, almost 4 km (2.5 miles) deep.

The cherub statue from the famous staircase has been brought up from the shipwreck.

plaque   stone or metal tablet in memory of the dead
sonar   using sound waves to detect objects under water

27

THE SHIP'S CAT

THE MYSTERY OF THE *JOYITA*

A 23-metre long fishing boat called the *Joyita* left an island in the Pacific in 1955 with 25 people on board. The boat was made with cork to stop it from sinking. The pleasure trip to the Tokelau Islands should have taken under 48 hours, but the *Joyita* never arrived. Five weeks later a passing ship near Fiji spotted the *Joyita* 600 miles off course. It was adrift and deserted and the ship's **logbook** was missing. On deck there were blood-stained bandages. No trace of any of the passengers has ever been found. The *Joyita* is yet another mystery of the sea that is unlikely to be solved.

A cat lived on board the *Joyita*. It was seen on deck on the day the boat left on its last doomed voyage. The cat was jumpy. It ran along the deck then dashed down the plank onto dry land and disappeared. Could this have been an **omen**?

The mystery of the *Kursk* has not yet been explained.

logbook　official diary of a ship's voyage

THE MYSTERY OF THE *KURSK*

In August 2000, the world waited in fear when the Russian **nuclear submarine** *Kursk* sank. It could not rise up from the bed of the Barents Sea. 118 men were stuck inside, 100 metres down. This was a six-year-old submarine with all the latest hi-tech equipment. How could this happen?

MYSTERY EXPLOSIONS

Two explosions sent the submarine into the mud under the sea. The water down there was only 3 °C. Inside the *Kursk* it was pitch black and getting hotter all the time. Rescue teams rushed to the scene to try and help but it was hopeless. The *Kursk* could not be rescued and all the men on board died.

FOUND

One of the bodies found in the *Kursk* held a note that told how 23 men remained alive after the explosions killed most of the crew. It said, 'None of us can get to the surface. I am writing blindly.' They were the last words he wrote.

Families of the sailors on the *Kursk* throw flowers into the sea. ❱❱

nuclear submarine   submarine powered by nuclear power and carrying nuclear missiles

MYSTERY POWERS

THE NORTH WALL

The Gulf Stream is a current of warm water that runs along the east coast of the USA. It meets the cold Atlantic near Bermuda. 'The North Wall' is where the two areas of water meet. It can cause strange weather and freak waves. Maybe these waves wipe out small boats.

There are strange parts of the sea called Devil's Triangles. These are places where ships and planes often go missing. Islands lie at the three points of the triangles. The most famous is the Bermuda Triangle. Between Florida, Bermuda and Puerto Rico is the eerie Sargasso Sea. Hundreds of people have vanished here in the last 50 years. It can be deathly still, with thick seaweed and yellow mists. Or, in sudden storms, the sea can whip up and form heaving waves. Planes have fallen from the sky inside the Bermuda Triangle. Radios and compasses have stopped working. Are there strange powers at work? Or is it all just **myth** and unlucky **coincidence**?

The Sargasso sea looks harmless ... but mysteries lurk out there.

WEIRD WORDS   coincidence   two or more strange things that happen at the same time

MISSING SHIPS

Small boats disappear there each year. Maybe that is not surprising because the sea can be so stormy. But what about large ships going missing? In 1980, a 12,000-tonne cargo ship called the *Poet* disappeared with 34 crew on board. The ship had just passed all its safety checks. The last anyone heard of the *Poet* was when one of the crew called his wife on the ship-to-shore radio. He told her that all was well. The ship was at the edge of the Sargasso Sea and the weather was fine. Yet the *Poet* vanished soon after this and nothing was ever found. Such mysteries just cannot be explained.

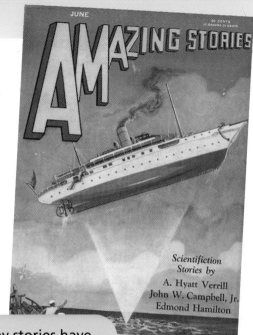

Many stories have been written about the Bermuda Triangle.

CHOPPY SEAS

Scientists can track tropical storms on radar to warn sailors about dangerous seas. But some storms can appear suddenly and destroy a boat quickly. The storms die down again before they show on radar. Wreckage is not often found, which is another mystery.

GAS

One idea to explain why some boats vanish is that gas bubbles up from the seabed. This gas may make patches of 'fizzy sea' that stop anything floating across. If a boat sails into a patch of gassy water like this, it will probably sink like a stone.

HOT ROCKS

Perhaps some of the odd things people see at sea can be explained by nature. Lights hovering on the waves at night could be flames. In some of the deep **trenches** under the ocean there are hot springs. **Vents** deep down on the **seabed** let out gas and fire. Smoking rocks **belch** out thick clouds of black smoke that rise up into the sea water. These smoke clouds can appear 4 kilometres (6 miles) under the water. They are very hot but when they reach the surface, they just give a puff of steam. No one on the sea would know about the fires deep down below.

Volcanoes at sea cause many strange effects.

An underwater vent may cause ships to sink.

belch   pass out gas noisily
erupt   burst out suddenly

BOILING SEA

It is only in the last few years that scientists have been able to go deep down to study **lava** flows on the ocean floor. Metals like copper and gold ooze up from the seabed and dissolve in the heat. Water jets from **volcanic** vents get hotter than 350 °C. Now and again a sudden burst of gas and fire shoots up from the seabed. If it hits the surface with a roar, a small boat could easily disappear. Could this explain why some boats vanish in parts of the Pacific Ocean? Undersea volcanoes often **erupt** in an area called the Pacific 'Ring of Fire'.

SOME LIKE IT HOT

Is there really life down there among the gas and fire? Amazingly, yes. Tubeworms live around the vents in piping hot water. They make tasty snacks for crabs – ready cooked! These creatures were first found in 1977.

We have only just discovered tubeworms. What else could be **lurking** down there?

lava   hot liquid rock that flows from a volcano
vent   hole that lets out gas and smoke, like a chimney

TSUNAMIS

If a large wave sweeps in from the sea, it can be bad news. In earthquake areas this can happen a lot. The sea around Japan has many of these freak waves called tsunamis.

Tsunamis are caused by earthquakes, landslides or volcanic eruptions at sea.

MAKING A SPLASH

The **Earth's crust** is thin in places, with many deep cracks. This is where earthquakes can happen. **Tremors** often lead to undersea landslides that shake up the sea. Big waves will then spread out from the middle of the **seaquake**. If the seabed **buckles** and bends, the water above will swirl and splash. The ocean floor can force great volumes of water upwards. This is enough to make a huge wave, like a moving wall of water. These waves are bad news for boats and bad news for people on the coast. Some of these 30-metre-high waves have crashed over land and killed hundreds of people.

buckle   twist and crumple
Earth's crust   layer of rock around the Earth

Date	Place	Cause and size	Deaths
February 1996	Biak, Irian Jaya	Earthquake. Waves 4.5 to 9 metres high	161
21 February 1996	North coast of Peru	Earthquake. Waves 5 metres high	12
17 November 1996	Near Brownsville, Texas, USA	Bad weather. Waves 3 metres high	10
17 July 1998	Papua New Guinea	Earthquake. Waves 7 to 15 metres high	3000
15 September 1999	Fatu Hiva, Marquesas Islands	Landslide. Two waves 5 metres high	No human lives lost

This table lists the most recent bad tsunamis. «

MAKING WAVES

In the open sea, a massive wave can move faster than 160 kilometres (100 miles) per hour. It slows down as it reaches the shore, but it is still fast if you are running away up the beach.

Such 'killer waves' are called **tsunamis**, from the Japanese *tsu* – 'port' and *nami* – 'wave'. They have killed thousands of people over the years. Approximately 60,000 people were killed in Portugal in 1755 by a giant wave. No one knew what caused tsunamis then. Once again people blamed the gods.

If a **meteorite** hits the sea, it will send a giant wave sweeping towards land. Scientists think this has happened in the past. The bigger the meteorite, the bigger the wave. Who knows when the next one will strike?

A tsunami in 1992, in South America, wrecked towns and killed 170 people. ∧∧

meteorite   large lump of rock, metal or ice from outer space
tremor   shaking caused by an earthquake

35

WATERSPOUTS

A **waterspout** is a tornado that moves over the sea like a whirlpool in the sky, sucking up water. It only lasts for 15 to 20 minutes. At 10 to 100 metres high, it spins at 20 to 80 metres per second. It could give a small boat a very hard time.

WHIRLPOOLS

When you pull out the bath plug you will see a mini **whirlpool** as the water swirls away. The same thing happens if an earthquake cracks a hole in the **seabed** and the sea pours down. Could some missing ships have been sucked down by a giant whirlpool? Such things may happen in the Bermuda Triangle.

GIANT SWIRLS

Strong currents and **tides** can also make whirlpools. There is a lot of mystery and **myth** surrounding them. Old Sow is the name of a whirlpool in New Brunswick, USA. Water swirls into the bay at Deer Island Point. Strong currents meet in undersea **trenches** and stir the sea into a **vortex**.

tide   daily rise and fall of the sea
vortex   mass of whirling fluid in a spiral

GREAT DANGER

Before the days of motor boats, Old Sow used to swallow up boats that could not get away. In 1835, two brothers sailed from Deer Island. Their mother watched in horror from the shore as their boat was sucked down. The men were never seen again.

THE MAELSTROM

In Arctic Norway there are two great whirlpools. They form something called the Maelstrom. Four times a day the tides rush over a narrow ledge of rock that spikes upwards from the seabed. The deep currents smash against the rock and meet surface water that is going even faster. This creates an area of angry sea that grinds up any ship that goes near it.

FIVE FAMOUS AND DEADLY WHIRLPOOLS

Some of the world's largest whirlpools include:
* the Corryvreckan, North Sea, Scotland. It is about a third of a kilometre across
* the Old Sow, New Brunswick, USA
* Naruto Whirlpool, Japan. This can be viewed from a highway bridge
* the Saltstraumen, Norway
* the Maelstrom, Norway.

Whirlpools swirl under Naruto bridge in Japan. >>

waterspout   twisting column of water and spray, like a tornado over the sea

SECRET LIFE

NASTY

The vampire squid is just a few centimetres long, but has the largest eyeballs of any animal compared to its body. It has wing-like fins and can turn tiny lights on and off all over its body. These help it to find **prey** in the dark sea at depths of several kilometres.

Some of the biggest mysteries of our planet take place deep under the sea. There are many undiscovered creatures down there in **trenches** and caves. Others have only been **glimpsed**. These creatures cannot **survive** at the surface. We need special deep-sea submarines and robot cameras to see them. We are only just beginning to explore the deepest corners of the oceans. Most fish in the deep ocean are blind. It is so dark that they do not need to see. Some of them are able to make their own light and glow. They have to **adapt** to great pressure and cold, too. In fact, it is a **hostile** world down there.

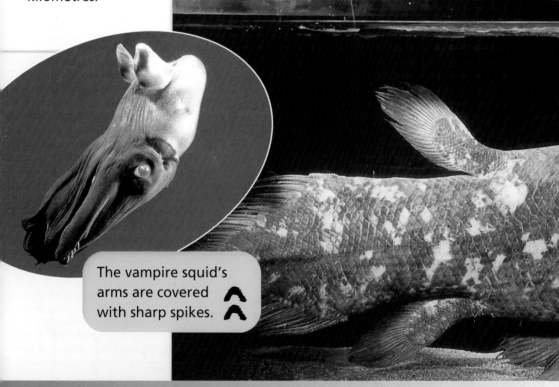

The vampire squid's arms are covered with sharp spikes.

WEIRD WORDS   adapt   change or adjust to new surroundings
glimpse   just a quick look

STILL UNKNOWN

So far, scientists have recorded over 25,000 **species** of fish and they think the deep may hold another ten million species! That is more species than are known to live on land.

LIVING DINOSAUR

For years, scientists knew about a fossil fish. The last coelacanth (pronounced *see-la-kanth*) was thought to have died out 80 million years ago. It was a large, man-sized fish. Then, in 1938, someone caught a live one. They said it was like 'finding a live dinosaur roaming the Earth'. More have been found since. In 1997 a scientist saw one in a fish market in Indonesia. The biggest so far weighed about 95 kilograms and was about 1.8 metres long.

LITTLE MONSTER

The angler fish looks scary. It has a tiny glowing light that hangs above its head. This attracts prey, which soon meet a nasty end in the angler's fanged jaws. This black fish is only the size of a baby's fist. Hopefully there are no bigger angler fish **lurking** down there.

The coelacanth is still out there.

prey   victim to be killed and eaten
species   type or sort of living thing

HEAD FOUND IN SHARK

Fishermen had a shock in 2001 when they caught a tiger shark off Australia's east coast. When they cut open the 4-metre long shark, a human head rolled out. The police had a mystery on their hands. Whoever he was, the victim had probably drowned before the shark ate his head whole.

HUNTERS

We already know about 400 different types of shark, but there could be many more living in the depths of the oceans. We still know very little about sharks.

SUPERFISH

Sharks are some of the oldest creatures on the Earth. They first appeared 400 million years ago, that is about 200 million years before dinosaurs. They do not seem to get diseases like some fish, as they have a strong **immune** system.

Sharks do an important job. They are rubbish collectors and get rid of ill or weak fish. They get a bad name from the few sharks that attack people. Most sharks are harmless to humans.

More people are killed each year by bee stings than by sharks.

immune   protected against disease

MONSTERS

In the last few years, people have seen Pacific sharks even larger than great white sharks. They may grow to over 10 metres long. They live so far down that they are not likely to be a threat to humans.

BIG FISH

The biggest living fish is the whale shark. It can grow up to 15 metres long and can weigh 15 tonnes. It feeds on **plankton** and does not harm humans. It is thought to live for up to 150 years.

In 1918, fishermen near Sydney, Australia, reported seeing a monster of a shark take their crayfish pots. They said the shark was 35 metres long. That really *is* a monster mystery.

ONCE BITTEN, TWICE UNLUCKY!

A shark once had its own mystery to sort out. In 1968, Henry Bource was filming sharks near Melbourne when one bit off his leg. Luckily for him it took his false leg. He had worn it since he lost his real leg to another shark.

The whale shark is the world's largest fish.

There are only 50 to 75 reported shark attacks in the world each year.

plankton   very tiny shrimp-like organisms that float in the sea

MEGALODON

Large teeth from the Megalodon shark have been found and dated at just 11,000 years old. That is not very long ago, compared to the millions of years the shark has been around. Is it just possible that the Megalodon **survived** to modern times?

LARGE KILLERS

There could be a monster twice the size of a great white shark deep in the oceans. Whether this huge creature still exists is still a mystery. A great white shark is scary enough at 8 metres long. The film *Jaws* gave this powerful creature a bad name. Everyone saw it as a deadly man-eater. So what would they make of its **ancestor**?

MONSTER SHARK

Skeletons and jaws have been found that belong to a monster shark. It was called Megalodon. Although it may have been **extinct** for many years, some people believe these 'eating machines' could still be out there. Scientists have yet to solve the mystery.

The film *Jaws* used a fake shark.

The size of its teeth show that the Megalodon was three times as big as a great white shark.

ancestor   relative from the past
extinct   died out, never to return

MEGAMOUTH

Can there really be large sharks we have not yet seen deep in the sea? In 1976 the US navy caught a 1-tonne shark. No one had seen a creature like this before. They called it a Megamouth. Since then about twelve more have been found. Three fishermen caught one in the Philippines in 1998. The Megamouth is very rare and does not harm humans. Like the gentle whale shark, its huge mouth is for sifting **plankton** from the sea.

The first female Megamouth was washed up on a beach in South Africa in 2002. She was about 4 metres long. Scientists were thrilled to find her – but still **mystified**.

WHAT THE EXPERTS SAY

Megamouth behaves like other fish of the deep ocean. It swims at depths of 200 metres by day, and just 15 metres at night. It flees from any noise into deep trenches, which may explain why this shark has kept hidden for so long.

The megamouth shark is harmless to humans just like this basking shark. **‹‹**

mystified   puzzled and baffled

GIANT FACTS AND FIGURES

The world's largest known sea creatures include:

Largest fish	Whale shark. Record of 30 metres long.
Largest jellyfish	Over 2 metres across the bell with a **tentacle** 40 metres long.
Largest **carnivore**	Great white shark. Record of 9 metres long, over 2 tonnes.

There may well be bigger creatures out there that we have not found yet.

OCEAN GIANTS

Science fiction stories are full of giant sea creatures that attack any diver in sight. A giant crab may rip apart a human in a horror film, but can it happen in real life? The sea's giants have always amazed us.

A giant spider crab's body can be 30 centimetres across. A crab this big would weigh about 6.5 kilograms, and have a leg span of 4 metres. It may not be able to tear a victim apart, but it could give quite a nasty nip.

There are huge clams in the South Pacific. They can grow up to 1.2 metres across. Although they have been given the name 'man-eating clam', they shut too slowly to trap a diver.

A giant jellyfish off the coast of the USA.

science fiction made-up stories that may twist the facts of science

THE TRUE GIANT

The blue whale is the largest mammal on the Earth. It can reach 30 metres long and can weigh up to 200 tonnes. Its heart is the size of a car. Blue whales feed on **plankton** and are harmless to humans. They are now rare and in danger because they are hunted for their oil. A single blue whale could make 120 barrels of oil. In 1931, over 29,000 were killed in one season.

The real mystery of these magnificent creatures is how they 'talk' to each other across hundreds of kilometres of ocean. They seem to have their own language of rumbles and clicks. Whales are some of the most intelligent creatures on the Earth.

A STORY OF A MAN-EATER

In 1891 James Bartley was whaling off the Falklands. He fell overboard and was swallowed by a sperm whale. Two days later the whale was caught and cut open. Bartley was in the whale's stomach, just alive. His skin was bleached white. Somehow he recovered.

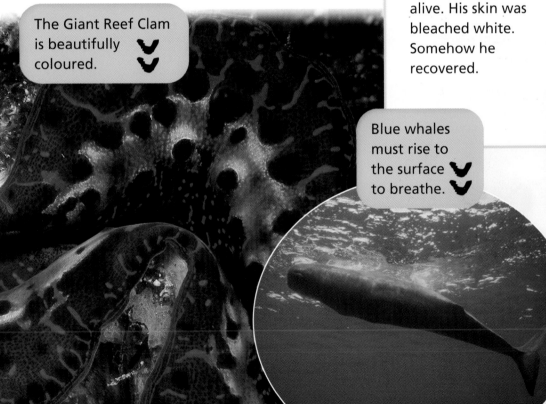

The Giant Reef Clam is beautifully coloured.

Blue whales must rise to the surface to breathe.

tentacle   long arm of a squid or octopus

TEN TENTACLES

It is a mystery how large giant squid can grow so huge. The longest tentacles seen so far stretched to over 20 metres. Could giant squid eat humans? It is possible. Some stories mention such attacks. We cannot go down to its deep-sea home and we have no idea where to find it, so how will we ever really know?

GIANT SQUID

Of all the creatures in the sea, perhaps the most mysterious is the giant squid. We know so little about it. That is because so few have been seen alive. They live very deep down, but sometimes they get washed up on beaches. Some are known to be longer than two buses.

ATTACK

In 1941 the Germans sank a British ship in the Atlantic. Suddenly a giant squid came to the surface. It wrapped a **tentacle** around one man and pulled him under. He was not seen again. Then a tentacle grabbed another man's leg. The suckers on its tentacles pulled his skin and left ulcers. He was rescued but his legs were scarred for years.

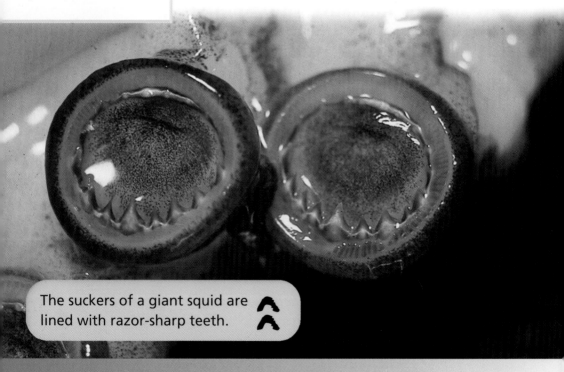

The suckers of a giant squid are lined with razor-sharp teeth.

skipper   person in charge of a boat

MONSTER SQUID GRIPS RACING YACHT

In 2003, a yacht in the Jules Verne round-the-world sailing competition met with mystery. The yacht was suddenly gripped by giant arms for over an hour in the mid-Atlantic.

'The giant squid was pulling really hard. I've been sailing for 40 years, and I've never seen anything like it', said the **skipper**.

One of the French crew saw the creature through a porthole. 'The arms were as thick as mine in an oil-skin. I thought of the damage it could do. When we saw it behind the boat it must have been 9 metres long,' he said. Many people thought the sailors must have been mistaken.

Giant squid have a parrot-like beak, eight arms and two long tentacles to grab food.

20,000 LEAGUES UNDER THE SEA

Jules Verne was a writer of **science fiction**. In 1868 he wrote this famous story set under the sea. A giant squid had a fight with a submarine. Captain Nemo and his *Nautilus* crew battled with the mystery monster.

FROM MYSTERY TO KNOWLEDGE

EARLY FINDS

Only since the 19th century have scientists discovered animals and plants living at great depths.

1818: Sir John Ross lowers a line a kilometre under the sea and finds worms and a starfish.

1843: Edward Forbes says no life can exist below 600 metres.

1872-76: Challenger lowers gear into the deep, finding hundreds of unknown animals.

Each year we discover new facts about sea life. The oceans are slowly revealing some of their dark secrets.

People have only been able to go deep under the sea in the last 50 years. In 1960, a mini-submarine dived 11 kilometres (6 miles) down for the first time in history. Three years later it found an American submarine that had sunk 2 kilometres (1.2 miles) down with the loss of 129 men.

Deep-sea exploring solved more mysteries in the 1980s. American teams travelled several kilometres down in a submarine called *Alvin*. They saw **volcanic vents** that blew out clouds of black smoke and water hot enough to melt lead.

Modern submarines can reach great depths.

A robotic arm on a submarine was used to collect things from the *Titanic* wreck.

WEIRD WORDS   the bends sickness caused by coming up from a deep dive too quickly

EXPLORING BELOW

In 1988, treasure hunters dived down more than a kilometre near South Carolina, USA. They found a wooden ship that had sunk in 1857. The ship was full of gold. Robert Ballard, the famous scientist and deep-sea diver, has found **ancient** ships deep in the Mediterranean. One was a 4th-century Roman ship.

In 1993, Japan began work on Kaiko – the world's deepest-diving camera robot. Kaiko has since dived to depths of over 11 kilometres (6 miles). Its pictures showed that the eerie darkness was alive with small animals.

In 1997 a robot called *Odyssey* first went down to look for giant squid in the dark water off New Zealand. The search for mysterious deep-sea creatures has only just begun…

The bends used to be a real mystery for divers. Now they spend time in **decompression chambers** to avoid getting ill. **>>**

THE BENDS

Divers years ago took great risks. When divers come up to the surface too fast, the change in pressure can form gas bubbles in their blood. Many got ill from **the bends** and some died.

decompression chamber   room that brings a diver back to normal pressure very slowly

FACTS AND FIGURES

Can it really be true?

- 80 per cent of all life on the Earth is found under the ocean.

- 97 per cent of the Earth's water is saltwater ocean.

- 85 per cent of this is the cold deep sea below 3.8 kilometres (2.5 miles).

- 90 per cent of all **volcanic** activity occurs in the oceans.

And we have hardly seen any of it yet.

MYSTERIES SOLVED

We are just on the brink of major discoveries. Who knows what we might find deep down in the sea? We may find the enormous creatures that the sailors of long ago talked about.

In the deepest parts of the ocean, the pressure is roughly 12,400 tonnes per square metre. That is like one person trying to hold up 50 jumbo jets. Yet tiny creatures live there that we have not even met yet.

We have not even discovered all the mysteries of the Great Barrier **Reef** in Australia. At 2000 kilometres (1250 miles) long, it is the largest living structure on the Earth. It can even be seen from the Moon.

Building under the sea has started already. This is an underwater hotel in Florida, USA.

THE SEARCH GOES ON

The sea will always be a world of mystery. Even so, we will keep trying to solve many of its riddles. What will we find in the next few years?

- Are the wrecks of missing planes and boats still out there?
- Clues to Atlantis and other lost worlds?
- The truth behind the Bermuda Triangle and its powers?
- How many new sea creatures will we discover?
- Will huge sea **serpents** be filmed for the first time?
- Will we save the sea from over-fishing, pollution and destruction?
- Will we live and work in buildings under the sea?

These are just some of the questions we hope to answer in the near future.

THE DEEP OF THE FUTURE

One of the big mysteries facing the future of our planet is how much deeper 'the deep' will get. On average, the sea has risen 10 to 25 centimetres over the past 100 years. If the world's ice caps melt, the sea will rise another 66 metres. We may have to live under the sea ourselves one day. This could be the biggest mystery of the deep in the future.

What mysteries still lurk in the planet's great oceans? **‹‹**

FIND OUT MORE

WEBSITES

SHARK TRUST
Information about sharks and their conservation.
sharktrust.org

BERMUDA TRIANGLE
History of the Triangle and lists of all the boats and planes that went missing there.
bermudatriangle.org

MARINE BIO
Find out about the weirdest sea creatures on this massive site.
marinebio.com

BOOKS
Can Science Solve? The Mystery of Atlantis, C. Oxlade and A. Ganeri (Heinemann Library, 1999)
Can Science Solve? The Mystery of the Bermuda Triangle, C. Oxlade and A. Ganeri (Heinemann Library, 1999)
Incredible Fish, John Townsend (Raintree, 2004)
Secret World of Whales, Theresa Greenaway (Raintree, 2003)

WORLD WIDE WEB
If you want to find out more about mysteries of the deep, you can search the Internet using keywords like these:

- 'Bermuda Triangle'
- 'megamouth shark'
- coelacanth
- Titanic + wreck
- ocean + mysteries
- whirlpools
- giant squid

You can make your own keywords using headings or words from this book.

SEARCH TIPS

There are billions of pages on the Internet so it can be difficult to find exactly what you are looking for. For example, if you just type in 'water' on a search engine like Google, you will get a list of 19 million web pages. These search skills will help you find useful websites more quickly:

- Use simple keywords, not whole sentences

- Use two to six keywords in a search

- Be precise – only use names of people, places or things

- If you want to find words that go together, put quote marks around them, for example 'giant squid' or 'sea creatures'

- Use the advanced section of your search engine

- Use the + sign to add certain words, for example typing + KS3 into the search box will help you find web pages at the right level.

WHERE TO SEARCH

SEARCH ENGINE

A search engine looks through the entire web and lists all the sites that match the words in the search box. The best matches are at the top of the list, on the first page. Try searching with **bbc.co.uk/search**

SEARCH DIRECTORY

A search directory is like a library of websites. You can search by keyword or subject and browse through the different sites like you would look through books on a shelf. A good example is **yahooligans.com**

GLOSSARY

adapt   change or adjust

ancestor   relative from the past

ancient   from a long time ago
in history

belch   pass out gas noisily

buckle   twist and crumple

capacity   number that can fit
onboard

carnivore   meat eater

coincidence   two or more strange
things that happen at the same time

continent   large land mass – bigger
than an island

coral   hard undersea growth around
tiny sea creatures

curse   words that bring about
supernatural powers and evil

decompression chamber   room that
brings a diver back to normal
pressure very slowly

dread   fear

Earth's crust   layer of rock around
the Earth

erupt   burst out suddenly

extinct   died out, never to return

fate   power that controls what
will happen

fleet   large group of ships

flounder   struggle

folklore   old beliefs, myths
and stories

funnel   large metal chimney

glimpse   just a quick look

Hindu   belonging to the ancient
Indian religion of Hinduism

hostile   unfriendly or against you

immune   protected against disease

jinx   unlucky force

larva   young creature just after it
has hatched

lava   hot liquid rock that flows from
a volcano

legend   story from long ago that
may be partly true

log book   official diary of a
ship's voyage

looted   raided

lurking   waiting around, ready
to strike

maiden voyage   first journey

mane   long hair growing down
the neck

mermaid   sea creature with the
body of a beautiful woman and the
tail of a fish

meteorite   large lump of rock, metal
or ice from outer space

mystified   puzzled and baffled

myth   made-up tale, told over time

New World   the Americas, which
were just being discovered

nuclear submarine submarine powered by nuclear power and carrying nuclear missiles

omen sign of good or evil

phantom ghost

plankton very tiny shrimp-like organisms that float in the sea

plaque stone or metal tablet in memory of the dead

prey victim to be killed and eaten

psychic able to see the future and show unusual powers of the mind

reef ridge of rock or coral near the surface of the sea

retired no longer in active service

rock formation natural feature made by the wearing away or movement of rock

rumour story based on gossip

science fiction made-up stories that may twist the facts of science

seabed bottom of the sea

seaquake earthquake under the sea

serpent like a large snake

siren creature in Greek myths whose singing attracted sailors

skipper person in charge of a boat

sonar using sound waves to detect objects under water

soul spirit of a person or place that is said to last forever

spawn lay many eggs

species type or sort of living thing

stone tablets slabs of stone that are carved with writing

superstition belief based on faith in the supernatural

survive stay alive despite the dangers

tentacle long arm of a squid or octopus

the bends sickness caused by coming up from a deep dive too quickly

tide daily rise and fall of the sea

torpedo cigar-shaped underwater missile

trance sleep-like state

tremor shaking caused by an earthquake

trench deep ditch, gully or valley

tsunami very large wave caused by an earthquake

UFO Unidentified Flying Object

vent a hole that lets out gas and smoke, like a chimney

Vikings Norwegian sailors and pirates from the 8th to 11th century

volcanic to do with a volcano

vortex mass of whirling fluid in a spiral

waterspout twisting column of water and spray, like a tornado over the sea

whaling ship ship for hunting whales

whirlpool powerful circular current

INDEX